GWENDOLYN MARTIN

Fort Myers & Fort Myers Beach Travel Guide

Discover Top Attractions, Restaurants & Activities

Copyright © 2023 by Gwendolyn Martin

All rights reserved. No part of this publication may be reproduced, stored or transmitted in any form or by any means, electronic, mechanical, photocopying, recording, scanning, or otherwise without written permission from the publisher. It is illegal to copy this book, post it to a website, or distribute it by any other means without permission.

Gwendolyn Martin asserts the moral right to be identified as the author of this work.

Gwendolyn Martin has no responsibility for the persistence or accuracy of URLs for external or third-party Internet Websites referred to in this publication and does not guarantee that any content on such Websites is, or will remain, accurate or appropriate.

Designations used by companies to distinguish their products are often claimed as trademarks. All brand names and product names used in this book and on its cover are trade names, service marks, trademarks and registered trademarks of their respective owners. The publishers and the book are not associated with any product or vendor mentioned in this book. None of the companies referenced within the book have endorsed the book.

First edition

This book was professionally typeset on Reedsy.
Find out more at reedsy.com

Contents

1. Introduction — 1
2. About Fort Myers — 3
3. About Fort Myers Beach — 5
4. Weather: The Sun Splashed Climate — 7
5. Journeying by Road and Air — 9
6. Renting a Car — 11
7. Where to Stay — 14
8. Top Restaurants — 17
9. Golfing — 26
10. Beaches, Parks and Water activities — 36
11. Excursions — 46
12. Boat Rental, Jet Ski Rentals and Boat Charters — 49
13. Entertainment and Activities — 51
14. Shopping — 58
15. Resources — 63
16. Conclusion — 64

1

Introduction

Warm greetings from the heart of Fort Myers & Fort Myers Beach! I'm Gwendolyn Martin, though you can call me Gwen, and I'm thrilled to guide you through a treasure trove of my favored activities and spots in our delightful area. Imagine having a compact, pocket-sized companion book to accompany you or a gift to your loved ones as you navigate our charming locale.

Having called Southwest Florida my home since 1991, after trading the brisk Ohio winters for Florida's inviting warmth, I've become intimately acquainted with the allures this area has to offer. My journey here has been as a resident and as a Realtor since my arrival, enabling me to explore and uncover the true gems of our region.

Whether you're embarking on a brief vacation, adopting the snowbird lifestyle (spending six sun-soaked winter months with us), or becoming a full-time resident, this book is your guide. While our beautiful beaches and invigorating water activities are often a primary draw, I assure you that more awaits your discovery. Allow this guide to be your starting point, inspiring you to dive in and fall as deeply in love with the area as I have. Consider this your brief, get-started guide to everything enchanting about Fort Myers.

In this book, I frequently reference "season" and "off-season." Our region's "season" spans from November through April, while "off-season" covers May to October. A primary distinction between the two is cost. For instance, hotel accommodations during the season are pricier compared to the off-season rates. The same applies to golfing in our locale. Off-season rates might range between $40 to $60, but during the peak season, these can surge from $80 to well over $200 for a round of 18 holes. That's what I'm referring to when I mention "season" versus "off-season."

Inside these pages, a world of activities unfolds, showcasing the best in dining, shopping, golfing, boating, entertainment, water adventures, and so much more in our vibrant area. Let's embark on this exploration journey together!

2

About Fort Myers

Fort Myers is a gem that is nestled along the Caloosahatchee River on Florida's Gulf Coast, Fort Myers is a sun-drenched paradise that seamlessly marries its rich history with modern-day attractions.

Historic Roots:

Thomas Edison and Henry Ford, two of America's most notable inventors, were among Fort Myers' early winter residents. They were drawn to its balmy climate and serene environment. Today, their estates stand as a testament to their time in Fort Myers, transformed into museums that give visitors a glimpse into their genius and lives in this tropical haven.

Natural Beauty:

Fort Myers' natural attractions are, without doubt, one of its biggest lures. The nearby beaches, like Fort Myers Beach and Sanibel Island, boast soft white sands and are often considered among the best in Florida. The area also has diverse wildlife, with manatees frequently spotted in its waters. For those with a keen interest in ecology, the Six Mile Cypress

Slough Preserve offers guided wetland tours, providing insights into the rich ecosystems of Southwest Florida.

Culture and Arts:

Downtown Fort Myers, often called the River District, showcases the city's cultural heart. Here, visitors can experience Art Walks, Music Walks, and many dining establishments that offer culinary delights ranging from local seafood to international cuisines. The Sidney & Berne Davis Art Center is a hub for the arts, hosting various events, exhibitions, and performances throughout the year.

Events and Festivals:

Fort Myers has various annual events that draw locals and tourists alike. From the Edison Festival of Light, which celebrates the city's connection to Thomas Edison, to the Shrimp Festival on Fort Myers Beach, there's always something happening in this vibrant city.

Gateway to Adventure:

The city also serves as a launching point for various adventures. Whether you're keen on exploring the nearby Everglades, indulging in water sports, or setting sail for a sunset cruise on the Gulf of Mexico, Fort Myers is the ideal base for it all.

With its historic charm, natural beauty, cultural attractions, and proximity to other notable Florida destinations, Fort Myers promises an experience that's as diverse as it is delightful. Whether you're a nature lover, history buff, beachgoer, or foodie, Fort Myers has something for everyone.

3

About Fort Myers Beach

Fort Myers Beach is situated on Estero Island and hugged by the waters of the Gulf of Mexico, Fort Myers Beach is a shimmering jewel of Southwest Florida. This tropical haven beckons visitors with its pristine sandy shores, captivating sunsets, and a laid-back vibe that's distinctly its own.

Azure Waters and Golden Sands:
One of the standout features of Fort Myers Beach is its expansive coastline, characterized by powdery white sands and tranquil azure waters. The gentle slope of the beach makes it ideal for families, swimmers, and those looking to simply bask in the sun. The soft sands also serve as a perfect canvas for castle-building enthusiasts and beachcombers seeking unique shells.

Times Square:
At the heart of Fort Myers Beach lies Times Square, which was a lively pedestrian district dotted with boutiques, eateries, and street performers. With its tropical palm trees, colorful establishments, and the melodic backdrop of live music, it's the go-to spot for evening entertainment

and dining. Presently, Times Square is undergoing renovations due to the damage caused by Hurricane Ian in 2022.

Watersports and Adventure:
The surrounding waters offer a plethora of activities. Kayaking, jet skiing, parasailing, and paddleboarding are just a few of the adventures awaiting the intrepid traveler. For those looking to dive deeper, snorkeling and scuba diving excursions reveal a fascinating underwater world teeming with marine life.

Eco-Tours and Wildlife:
The back bay areas of Fort Myers Beach are a sanctuary for diverse wildlife. Dolphins playfully skim the waters, while manatees, often referred to as 'sea cows', can be observed in their serene natural habitats. Boat tours and guided kayak trips offer a chance to get up close with these magnificent creatures while learning about the rich ecosystems of the region.

Festive Spirit:
Fort Myers Beach hosts various events throughout the year, such as the Sand Sculpting Championship, which draws artists from around the world to showcase their sand-sculpting prowess. Another notable event is the Shrimp Festival, celebrating the town's fishing heritage with parades, food stalls, and plenty of community spirit.

A Retreat for All:
Whether you're seeking a romantic getaway, a family vacation, or a solo retreat to reconnect with nature, Fort Myers Beach provides a picturesque backdrop for unforgettable memories. Its blend of natural beauty, recreational activities, and warm hospitality ensures that every visitor leaves with a piece of this coastal paradise etched in their heart.

4

Weather: The Sun Splashed Climate

Located in Southwest Florida, Fort Myers & Fort Myers Beach area enjoys a tropical Savannah climate, ensuring it remains a year-round destination for both residents and visitors. Here's a closer look at its enticing weather patterns:

Warm Winters:

One of the prime attractions of Fort Myers and Fort Myers Beach is its pleasantly warm winters. While much of the United States grapples with snow and cold, Fort Myers boasts average daytime temperatures in the mid-70s (°F) during these months. This makes it an ideal retreat for "snowbirds" looking to escape chillier climates.

Balmy Summers:

Summer in Fort Myers and Fort Myers Beach is characterized by hot, humid conditions, with temperatures often soaring into the 90s (°F). It's also the wet season, with regular afternoon thunderstorms providing a refreshing reprieve from the heat. These storms are typically brief but intense, often followed by brilliant rainbows arching across the sky.

Gulf Breezes:

Benefiting from its proximity to the Gulf of Mexico, Fort Myers and Fort Myers Beach often experience gentle sea breezes, especially during the late afternoon. These breezes not only make the heat more bearable but also add a certain charm to beachside evenings.

Hurricane Season:

Like much of Florida, Fort Myers and Fort Myers Beach are susceptible to hurricanes, with the season typically spanning from June to November. While the city has witnessed its share of storms, modern infrastructure, vigilant weather monitoring, and effective evacuation plans ensure the safety of its residents and visitors.

In summary, Fort Myers and Fort Myers Beach offer a delightful blend of sun-soaked days, balmy evenings, and occasional tropical rain showers. Its consistent warmth and abundant sunshine make it a magnet for those seeking the quintessential Floridian experience. Whether you're lounging on its beaches, exploring its natural parks, or just strolling downtown, Fort Myers and Fort Myers Beach weather is often as welcoming as its residents.

5

Journeying by Road and Air

Tucked away on the southwestern edge of Florida, Fort Myers serves as a serene retreat along the banks of the Caloosahatchee River near the expansive Gulf of Mexico. Its position on the map makes it a strategic stopover for those exploring the Sunshine State.

By Road

From Miami: Fort Myers is roughly a two-hour drive away from the bustling streets of Miami. Traveling westward on the I-75, one can enjoy the changing landscapes, from urban skyscrapers to the tranquil wetlands of the Everglades, leading to the coastal beauty of Fort Myers.

From Orlando: A drive from the theme park capital, Orlando, to Fort Myers, spans approximately three hours. One would primarily use the I-4 and then the I-75 South, passing through a mix of Florida's inland towns, verdant farmlands, and scenic highways.

From Tampa: Located north, Tampa is a straightforward drive of around two hours via the I-75 South. The journey offers a glimpse of Florida's west coast, with its lush landscapes and opportunities for spontaneous detours to lesser-known beaches or nature reserves.

By Air

Fort Myers is well-serviced by the Southwest Florida International Airport (RSW) for those looking to save time or coming from distant locales. Major airlines operate frequent flights, connecting Fort Myers with cities across the U.S. and beyond. The airport's location, a mere 20-minute drive from downtown, ensures convenience for travelers.

Fort Myers location makes it both an accessible destination and a strategic launching pad for broader Floridian adventures. Whether you're coming from the energetic vibes of Miami, the magical allure of Orlando, or the bay-side charm of Tampa, Fort Myers offers a warm welcome to all.

6

Renting a Car

Rental Agencies

Given Fort Myers' popularity as a vacation destination, all major rental car agencies operate in the area. Companies like Enterprise, Hertz, Alamo, Avis, Budget, and National have facilities at the Southwest Florida International Airport (RSW) and various locations throughout the city.

Booking in Advance

It's advisable to reserve a car in advance, especially during peak travel times like winter and spring break. Not only will this ensure availability, but you may also get better rates than booking on the spot.

Picking Up

If you're flying into Fort Myers, the most convenient location to pick up your rental car is at Southwest Florida International Airport (RSW). The Rental Car Center is located on airport property and provides direct access to Interstate 75. Shuttle services are available to take passengers from the terminal to the Rental Car Center.

Age Restrictions

Typically, the minimum age to rent a car is 21. However, renters between the ages of 21 and 24 may encounter additional fees. Some rental companies might have a higher age minimum for certain vehicle types.

Documentation

You'll need a valid driver's license to rent a car. International visitors should also have an International Driving Permit if their license isn't in English. Most rental companies will also require a credit card for security purposes.

Insurance

When renting a car, you'll be offered various insurance options, such as collision damage waivers or liability coverage. Check in advance with your credit card company or personal auto insurance, as you might already have coverage that extends to rental cars.

Navigating

While Fort Myers is relatively easy to navigate, having a GPS system can be beneficial, especially if you plan to explore beyond the city. Many rental companies offer GPS devices as an add-on, or you can use smartphone apps like Google Maps or Waze.

Returning

Ensure you're aware of the fuel policy. Some companies require you to return the car with a full tank, while others might allow you to pre-purchase fuel.

Local Traffic Laws

Always familiarize yourself with local traffic laws. In Florida, for

RENTING A CAR

instance, it's mandatory to stop for school buses when they're picking up or dropping off children. U-turns are allowed at intersections unless there's a sign indicating otherwise.

Renting a car in Fort Myers offers you the freedom and flexibility to explore the city and its surrounding areas at your own pace. Whether you're planning a trip to nearby beaches, nature preserves, or cities, having a rental car enhances the experience.

7

Where to Stay

Fort Myers, Florida, offers a range of accommodation options to suit different preferences and budgets. Here are some recommendations on where to stay, categorized by type:

Beachfront Resorts

If you're looking for a luxury experience with direct beach access, consider staying on Fort Myers Beach, which is a short drive from the downtown area.

- **Pink Shell Beach Resort & Marina**: Known for its stunning Gulf views, spa facilities, and water sports.
- **Diamond Head Beach Resort**: This resort offers spacious suites, a pool, on-site restaurants, and is located directly on the beach.

Historic Hotels

For those keen on experiencing the rich history of Fort Myers:

- **The Hibiscus House Bed & Breakfast**: Located downtown, it's a charming B&B that offers a slice of old Florida.

- **The Edison & Ford Winter Estates**: While it's primarily a historic site and museum, there are sometimes packages available that include stays in the nearby Marina Village, which offers condos and a lively marina setting.

Budget Accommodations

If you're traveling on a tighter budget:

- **Travelodge by Wyndham Fort Myers**: An affordable option with essential amenities.
- **La Quinta Inn & Suites by Wyndham Fort Myers Airport**: Convenient for those flying in or out, with a free airport shuttle.

Mid-Range Hotels

- **Holiday Inn Fort Myers - Downtown Area**: Centrally located with modern amenities.
- **Courtyard by Marriott Fort Myers Cape Coral**: Offers a pool, fitness center, and is conveniently located near major highways.

Vacation Rentals

Platforms like Airbnb or Vrbo offer a variety of rental options in Fort Myers, from beachfront condos to homes nestled in residential neighborhoods. This option is ideal if you prefer a more home-like setting or are traveling with a group.

- **Eco-Lodging:** For those who enjoy nature:
- **Manatee Park**: While it doesn't offer traditional lodging, it's a great place to camp and is known for its manatee viewing in the cooler months.

Boutique Inns:

- **Hotel Indigo Fort Myers Downtown River District**: This stylish, pet-friendly hotel is located in the heart of downtown Fort Myers, making it easy to explore local shops, restaurants, and entertainment.

When choosing where to stay, consider your priorities: beach access, proximity to attractions, budget, or specific amenities. Fort Myers offers a diverse range of accommodations to cater to the needs of its many visitors.

**PLEASE NOTE THAT IF YOU PLAN TO STAY IN OUR AREA FROM OCTOBER THROUGH APRIL, IT IS ADVISABLE TO MAKE RESERVATIONS 6 MONTHS TO A YEAR IN ADVANCE.

8

Top Restaurants

My husband and I thoroughly enjoy dining out, and we've compiled a list of our top 10 favorite restaurants. These selections are based on our preferences and influenced by various popular rankings. I chose restaurants that are not a chain but local to the Florida area. However, it's worth noting that the dining landscape can evolve, so consulting recent reviews or local suggestions is always wise. Here's our list:

The Veranda (Southern/American Food):
This elegant dining establishment has been a staple in downtown Fort Myers for years, offering Southern regional cuisine in a refined ambiance. You can enjoy your meal indoors or in the garden courtyard, surrounded by lush greenery that provides a breathtaking view. It's advisable to make reservations, and they accept seating from Monday to Saturday, 5 pm to 9 pm. Our favorites on the menu are the lamb chops and the table-side Caesar salad.

Address: 2122 Second Street, Fort Myers
 Phone: (239) 332-2065

Price range: $30 to $50
Website: https://verandarestaurant.com/

Cibo (Italian Food):

Cibo is known for its authentic Italian cuisine. Cibo has garnered a reputation for its gourmet pizzas, pasta, and extensive wine list. Cibo is a local family-owned restaurant whose service staff is amicable and good. They are open seven days a week. Sunday through Thursday, 4:00 pm to 9:00 pm. Friday & Saturday, they are available from 4:00 pm to 10:00 pm. They are closed on major holidays.

We make it a point to dine here monthly, and I'm particularly fond of their Spaghetti Alla Bolognese and the daily special of Mamma K's House-made ravioli. For starters, we often opt for the Ricotta Gnocchi, and for dessert, we split the Dark Chocolate Volcano Cake paired with Love Boat ice cream. My husband usually leans towards the specials, which never disappoints.

Address: 12901 McGregor Blvd, Fort Myers
Phone: (239) 454-3700
Price range: $20 to $50
Website: http://cibofortmyers.com/

Parrot Key Caribbean Grip (Seafood):

Parrot Key offers both indoor and scenic outdoor dining by the water, treating guests to the captivating vistas of the Back Bay. Their unique "Cockateils" are a hit, and their entrees, including Fish tacos, grouper, and Mahi, are must-tries. For those seeking entertainment, live performances are featured during the week. Their doors are open every day: Monday to Thursday from 11 am to 9 pm, Friday and Saturday from 11 am to 10 pm, and Sunday from 9 am to 9 pm.

Address: 2500 Main St, Fort Myers Beach
Phone: (239) 463-3257
Price range: $20 to $50
Website: https://www.myparrotkey.com/

El Gaucho Inca (Peruvian, Spanish, Argentinean, Latin Food):
This eatery offers a distinctive blend of Peruvian, Argentine, and Italian flavors, reflecting the city's rich culinary diversity with homemade preparations. Spearheaded by a local couple, it embodies the passion of a family-run venture. I invariably opt for the Tallarin Verde accompanied by Flank Steak, while my husband prefers the Trio Ceviche, a delightful combination of shrimp and fish. And, being dessert aficionados, we often indulge in the Mango Guava cheesecake or the Dulce de Leche. They welcome patrons from 3 pm to 9 pm on Tuesdays to Thursdays, 12 pm to 10 pm on Fridays and Saturdays, and 12 pm to 8 pm on Sundays. They've recently inaugurated a new branch in Estero.

Address: 4383 Colonial Blvd, Fort Myers, FL
Phone: (239) 275-7504
Price range: $15 to $50
Website: https://www.elgauchoinca.com/

Deep Lagoon Seafood and Oyster House (Seafood):
Tucked away in Florida's Heartland is a hidden gem where the beverages are refreshing, the seafood is straight from the ocean, and the dishes burst with flavor. Here, you can unwind, adopt a laid-back vibe, and immerse yourself in the authentic essence of "Real Florida". It's a haven from the hustle and bustle, a gathering spot for friends, and a locale filled with laughter and cherished memories. Deep Lagoon Seafood has several locations in Florida and is from the same family behind Pinchers restaurants. Deep Lagoon Seafood & Oyster Bar serves up the freshest

catch, sourced by local fishermen from nearby waters. They are open seven days a week from 11:00 am to 10:00 pm.

For appetizers, we're torn between the conch fritters, crab Rangoon, and gator bites—it's a challenge to settle on just one! Additionally, their New England Clam Chowder is an absolute must-have. When it's time for the main course, we're often drawn to their daily specials, which never disappoint. However, the Grouper Oscar, Chili-rubbed Tripletail, and Hogfish prepared lagoon-style frequently catch our eye. We've even sampled the blackened tripletail tacos, a delightful blend. And, if there's room to spare, we never miss out on a slice of their Key Lime pie.

Address: 14040 McGregor Blvd, Fort Myers
Phone: (239) 689-5474
Price range: $15 to $50
Website: https://www.deeplagoon.com/

The Lodge (Barbecue restaurant):

At The Lodge, every morsel you indulge in evokes the deep, smoky essence of dedicated grilling and marinating hours. Their iconic pulled pork, delicately flavored with mesquite and hickory, serenades your taste buds with its rich, savory melody. With their perfect char, the ribs offer a crunchy layer that unveils the juicy meat within, a testament to the art of slow cooking. The variety of sauces, ranging from a zesty apple-vinegar concoction to a bold molasses-infused creation, is tailored to enhance the dishes' natural goodness. Even the accompaniments stand tall in their own right, ensuring nothing is left in the backdrop. Dining here is not just about the food; it's an immersive journey into the soul of authentic barbecue craftsmanship.

On a recent visit, I brought my father along. He thoroughly enjoyed the outdoor seating, taking in the ambiance and watching the world go by, all while savoring the delicious offerings. Our go-to appetizer is always the Brisket Burnt Ends—a family favorite. My husband enjoys the combo plate, pairing the slow-smoked St. Louis Ribs with the flavorful brisket. As for me, I oscillate between the hearty Bison Burger and the Country Fried Steak sandwich. And of course, no meal is complete without dessert. The Reese's Peanut Butter Pie is unique in my heart, rounding off our culinary adventure perfectly. The hours are Sunday through Thursday from 11:00 am to 10:00 pm. Friday and Saturday are open from 11:00 am to 11:00 pm.

Address: 2278 First St, Fort Myers, FL
   Phone: (239) 433-2739
   Price range: $10 to $40
   Website: https://www.thelodgefl.com/

Cristof's on McGregor (American food):
   Cristof Danzi, a Sicilian native with extensive culinary training from Italy, France, England, and Bahrain, is the proud proprietor of Cristofs on McGregor, a quaint eatery nestled in Fort Myers, Florida. His inspiration stemmed from his father's culinary legacy. Housed in a beautifully preserved old home, the restaurant presents a harmonious blend of Southern and American cuisines, complemented by picturesque garden views. Guests can enjoy their meals indoors or relish the outdoor ambiance.

   Drawing from Mediterranean roots and fueled by a love for seafood, regional art, choice of aged beef, and iconic pasta creations, Cristof's establishment certainly delivers on its promise of an exceptional dining experience. Their curated wine selection pairs seamlessly with tantalizing starters, like the fried green tomatoes layered with bacon, fresh mozzarella, and a zesty roasted corn-jalapeno salsa, capturing the essence of southern Italian fare with a spicy twist. They welcome patrons from Monday to Saturday, offering lunch from 11:00 am to 3:00

pm and continuing service until 9:00 pm. Sundays are from 10:00 am to 8:30 pm.

Address: 10231 McGregor Blvd, Fort Myers
Phone: (239) 791-8473
Price range: $15 to $50
Website: https://cristofsonmcgregor.com/

San Luis Cuban Café Restaurant (Cuban & Latin):

If you're hunting for an authentic Cuban eatery around here, this spot is a must-visit. A cherished family-run establishment, it's slightly tucked away yet remains a local favorite. While they offer breakfast, my husband and I are regulars during lunchtime. I invariably choose the Ropa Viejas with rice, black beans, and tostones. Meanwhile, my husband can't resist the breaded steak accompanied by sweet plantains. Their Cubano sandwiches, café con leche, and guava pastries are also noteworthy. And our meal isn't complete without indulging in their creamy Flan. Their doors are open from 8:00 am to 5:30 pm on weekdays, extending to 6:00 pm on Saturdays, and they take a break on Sundays.

Address: 12995 S Cleveland Ave, Ft Myers
Phone: (239) 225-2822
Price range: $10 to $30

Origami (Korean, Sushi, Japanese Food):

Consistently celebrated for its excellence in Sushi, Korean, and Japanese dishes, Origami has garnered numerous accolades. Among these, the readers of Fort Myers' News Press have repeatedly voted it the Best Japanese Restaurant. As a cherished family establishment, the gratitude towards its loyal clientele in the Fort Myers community is immeasurable. Their unwavering support has enabled Origami to serve top-tier dishes to its treasured patrons continually.

Since 1994, Origami has been a culinary cornerstone in Southwest Florida, delivering the best of Asian cuisine. The menu boasts an array of Sushi, traditional Japanese and Korean dishes, and Korean BBQ, complemented by a full bar and extensive catering options. Hours are Monday through Saturday from 11:30 am to 9:00 pm and Sunday from 4:00 pm to 9:00 pm.

Depending on my current craving, I might opt for a Bento Box, offering a selection of 10 diverse choices, or gravitate towards the Bibimbap, a delightful mix of steamed rice crowned with beef, veggies, a fried egg, and sauce. When we're in the mood for rolls, we often find ourselves drawn to favorites like the Crazy Dragon, Scooby Doo, Black Russian, Hot Mango, PB & J Roll, Naruto, and the OMG roll. My daughter favors vegetable rolls like Sweet Potato, Avocado, Old School Vegetable, and Vegan Louisiana. We're pretty obsessed with their roll selection!

Address: 8911 Daniels Pkwy, Fort Myers, FL
Phone: (239) 482-2126
Price range: $12 to $40
Website: https://www.sushiorigami.com/

Ristorante Fabio Italian Restaurant (Italian):
We recently stumbled upon this hidden treasure and a word to the wise—secure a reservation during the peak season. This family-run establishment takes pride in serving cherished family recipes, with the daughters actively contributing to its success. On our visit, my husband decided to venture into their daily specials and was immensely satisfied with the Duck Wings Marmalade. This dish, reminiscent of the classic Duck a L 'Orange, surpassed our expectations. I opted for the Veal Marsala, which was impeccably prepared. Our culinary journey commenced with a sumptuous homemade seafood bisque brimming with clams, mussels, salmon, shrimp, calamari, and lobster. Capping

off our meal was the delicately airy Pumpkin Spice Tiramisu—a sweet conclusion to our delightful evening. They welcome guests from 4:00 pm to 9:00 pm, Wednesday to Saturday, and from 2:00 pm to 8:00 pm on Sundays.

Address: 4150 Hancock Bridge Pkwy, North Fort Myers
Phone: (239) 656-5727
Price range: $20 to $50
Website: https://ristorantefabio.com/

Love Boat (Icecream):

Love Boat Ice Cream in Fort Myers is a testament to timeless flavors and community bonds. Established in 1967, this beloved ice cream parlor has served generations of residents and visitors, offering a delightful array of creamy treats. For many, visiting Fort Myers is incomplete without indulging in a scoop or two from Love Boat. Its enduring presence over the decades speaks not only to the quality of its desserts but also to the cherished memories it has helped create. An emblem of sweet tradition, Love Boat Ice Cream continues to be a special destination for those seeking a nostalgic taste of Fort Myers' history. They offer over 50 flavors of icecream. Love Boat is open seven days a week from 11:00 am to 10:00 pm.

Address: 16475 San Carlos Blvd, Ft Myers, FL
Phone: (239) 466-7707
Website: https://loveboaticecream.com/

Wrap-up

Considering the ever-changing landscape of the restaurant scene, there's always the possibility of new establishments emerging or existing ones reinventing themselves. My husband and I have a long list of favored eateries, and our love for culinary exploration keeps growing. We're always eager to discover new dining spots and savor diverse dishes. To get the most updated insight on Fort Myers' dining options, perusing recent feedback on platforms such as Yelp, Trip Advisor, or Google Reviews is worthwhile.

9

Golfing

Southwest Florida, with its balmy weather, pristine beaches, and lush landscapes, is also home to some of the most captivating golf courses in the state. This region, stretching from Tampa Bay to the southern end of the Everglades, has firmly established itself as a must-visit destination for golf aficionados.

The courses here are diverse, ranging from meticulously manicured championship greens to more rustic courses that seamlessly blend with the natural environment. Many of these courses are designed by legendary golf architects like Jack Nicklaus, Arnold Palmer, and Tom Fazio, ensuring a world-class golfing experience.

Many of Southwest Florida's golf courses are part of larger resort communities, offering luxury amenities like top-tier clubhouses, professional training academies, and spa facilities. These establishments often host prestigious tournaments, drawing both national and international attention.

Beyond the courses themselves, the backdrop they're set against is truly awe-inspiring. From tranquil waterways teeming with local wildlife to panoramic views of the Gulf of Mexico, golfing in Southwest Florida is as much a communion with nature as it is a sport.

Moreover, the region's golfing community is vibrant and welcoming. Various leagues, clubs, and associations cater to all age groups and skill levels, fostering a culture of camaraderie and mutual respect. We also now have Top Golf and PopStroke featuring two 18-hole Tiger Woods designed putting courses.

Let's take a look at some of the fantastic golf courses in the area. Remember, prices do change, so always check online or call the golf course for the pricing.

PUBLIC GOLF COURSES

Eastwood Golf Course

Eastwood Golf Course owned and operated by the City of Fort Myers opened since September 1977 and designed by Robert Von Hagge and Bruce Devlin. Eastwood sits on the old city well field and comprises over 150 acres. It is located only 15 minutes from the SW Florida International Airport. It plays to a par 72 layout and possesses 87 strategically placed bunkers and water comes into play on 10 of the 18 holes. This course is very affordable. In the off season from May to October the fees run from $30 to $45 with season running a little higher. Open Monday through Friday from 6:00 am to 6:00 pm.

Address: 4600 Bruce Herd Lane
 Phone: (239) 321-7487
 Website: https://cityftmyers.com/1422/Eastwood-Golf-Course

Fort Myers Country Club

Situated along the iconic, palm-adorned McGregor Boulevard in Fort Myers, the Fort Myers Country Club Golf Course stands as a testament to the city's rich golfing heritage. Fondly referred to as "The Fort" by locals, this treasured course has been welcoming players since 1917. Crafted by the renowned architect Donald Ross in 1916, it stands as one of the West Coast of Florida's most historic golf venues. In the roaring 1920s, luminaries like Thomas Edison and Henry Ford were frequent visitors, given the course's proximity to their winter retreats. Boasting 18 meticulously designed holes, the course offers tee times from Monday to Friday between 6:00 am and 6:00 pm. While the fees range from $30 to $45 during the off-peak season, they tend to be slightly elevated during the peak period. For those seeking a delightful culinary experience after their game, the Edison Restaurant on the premises provides patio and indoor dining options for the public.

Address: 3591 McGregor Blvd, Fort Myers

Phone: (239) 321-7488
Website: https://www.cityftmyers.com/countryclub

Eagle Ridge Golf Club

Golf enthusiasts in Southwest Florida often regard Fort Myers as the pinnacle of their sport, and Eagle Ridge Golf Club stands as a testament to that reputation. This 6,500-yard championship course is beautifully woven into the native landscape, adorned with cypress and pine trees, and intertwined with numerous lakes and waterways. Indeed, with water playing a significant role in 17 out of the 18 holes, players of all skill levels are bound to face a challenging round. The course features a complete set of 18 holes.

Its prime location, a short drive from Southwest Florida International Airport, and the sun-kissed beaches of Fort Myers add to its allure. Ready to take on the challenge? Book your tee time and dive into the Eagle Ridge experience. Depending on the time of year, rates vary between $40 and $75 during the off-season and higher during the season, with available tee times from 7:00 am to 6:00 pm, every day of the week.

Address: 14589 Eagle Ridge Dr, Fort Myers
Phone: (239) 768-1888
Website: https://www.playeagleridge.com/

Old Corkscrew Golf Course

With his unparalleled commitment and creativity in golf course design, Jack Nicklaus has crafted some of the most captivating courses around the globe. Among these masterpieces, Old Corkscrew stands out as the sole Nicklaus Signature Design in Southwest Florida, earning its reputation as an essential golfing destination.

Spanning a magnificent 7,400 yards, this Championship Par 72 course upholds the pinnacle of design and upkeep standards. Distinctively, without being tethered to any real estate development, Old Corkscrew offers a pure, immersive golfing journey. The course offers nature enthusiasts a splendid opportunity to spot local wildlife, complemented by stunning vistas throughout its 18 holes.

Every nuance of the course harmoniously integrates with its natural surroundings, including the majestic oak, pine, and cypress trees, as well as the serene flow that traverses the heart of the property. This synergy culminates in a genuinely breathtaking golf experience. Tee times are available daily from 7:00 am to 5:00 pm, with rates ranging from $95 to $115 off-season and starting at $140 during the peak season.

Address: 17320 Corkscrew Rd, Estero
Phone: (239) 949-4700
Website: https://oldcorkscrew.com/

This list showcases only a fraction of the public golf courses available in our region, but there are many other courses to explore and enjoy. My husband and I are avid players and often find these courses challenging. Interestingly, we've found opportunities to play rounds at some exclusive private courses during the off-season, which usually spans May to October.

GOLFING

PRIVATE GOLF COURSES

The Southwest Florida region, specifically around Fort Myers, boasts an impressive collection of over 80 golf courses within just a 15-mile radius. This includes public greens and exclusive private courses. The area offers a diverse range of play, with 61 full 18-hole courses and 19 shorter 9-hole layouts. Given its rich golfing heritage and many courses, Southwest Florida has rightly earned its name as the "Golf Capital of the World". For a comprehensive list and details of the region's public and private courses, please refer to the provided Golf link link below. This will give you up-to-date golfing information for our area.

https://www.golflink.com/golf-courses/fl/fort-myers

ADVENTURE GOLF FOR FAMILIES

Top Golf

Topgolf Fort Myers stands as the pinnacle of entertainment in the Fort Myers, FL region. With its climate-controlled bays available throughout the year and HDTVs adorning every corner - from each bay to the vibrant sports bar and restaurant - it ensures a top-notch experience. Whether you're using the house clubs or bringing your own, the innovative technology incorporated into the outfield targets and balls does the scoring for you. More than just a golfing destination, Topgolf has revolutionized social interaction, merging technology and entertainment into a dynamic fusion. The energy here is palpable, making it a hub of activity any day you visit. The essence is not about perfecting your swing or setting high scores but about collective enjoyment. Beyond the game, the culinary offerings add zest to the experience. With their innovative takes on classic dishes, dining at Topgolf isn't just an afterthought – it's an essential part of the whole delightful experience. Operating hours are from 9:00 am to 11:00 pm from Sunday to Thursday. On Fridays and Saturdays, they are open from 9:00 am until midnight. Prices start at $30 an hour on up.

Address: 2021 Top Golf Way, Fort Myers
   Phone: (239) 933-2035
   Website: https://topgolf.com/us/fort-myers/

Pop Stoke

PopStroke offers a unique blend of technologically-enhanced golf combined with a casual dining experience. Based in Jupiter, Florida, this establishment boasts a team of experts specialized in food, beverage, and hospitality. As you navigate the course, you can indulge in an extensive selection of craft beers, wines, ice creams, and delicious meals. The incorporation of advanced tech, such as the PopStroke App and jumbotron leaderboard, amplifies the interactive and competitive feel of your golfing session. A highlight of the experience is the keepsake TaylorMade golf ball every guest receives. With two distinct 18-hole synthetic green courses, PopStroke caters to both seasoned golfers and families looking for a more relaxed round. Hours are Sunday through Thursday from 10:00 am to 11:00 pm. Friday and Saturday from 10:00 am to midnight. Prices start at $15 on up.

Address: 5531 Six Mile Commercial Ct, Fort Myers, FL 33912
Phone: (239) 323-4653
Website: https://popstroke.com/ft-myers-fl/

Miniature Golf – Castle Golf

GOLFING

Merging the charm of medieval times with a tropical paradise, Castle Golf offers a one-of-a-kind experience. Bask under the sun, let the sound of cascading waterfalls soothe you, and lose yourself amid verdant surroundings. Situated adjacent to Lakes Park, don't be surprised if you spot local wildlife adding a dash of mystery to your game. Some delightful residents have made the course their home, offering both entertainment and a chance for interaction. After a challenging 18 holes, satiate your hunger on their expansive patio or in the picnic areas. Operating hours are from 10:00 am to 10:00 pm, Sunday through Thursday, and from 10:00 am to 11:00 pm on Fridays and Saturdays. Prices start at $14 on up.

Address: 7400 Gladiolus Dr, Fort Myers
   Phone: (239) 489-1999
   Website: http://www.castle-golf.com/

10

Beaches, Parks and Water activities

Our beaches are truly spectacular. A frequent inquiry I receive is regarding the allowance of dogs on the shores. In Lee County, dogs are welcome on the beaches, provided they are leashed and under control. It's imperative to ensure they don't chase after the native wildlife. Kindly ensure they stay away from the nesting zones of birds, turtles, and other creatures.

Fort Myers Beach

Fort Myers Beach, located on Estero Island in Florida, boasts a stretch of soft, sugar-white sands that are caressed by the gentle waves of the Gulf of Mexico. This popular destination is not just a haven for sunbathers, but also attracts water sports enthusiasts, shell seekers, and nature lovers alike. The shoreline offers a serene backdrop of swaying palm trees and breathtaking sunsets that paint the horizon in hues of pink, orange, and purple. Beyond its scenic beauty, Fort Myers Beach hosts a plethora of seaside eateries, quirky shops, and vibrant events that cater to visitors of all ages. The nearby wildlife preserves and mangrove ecosystems further accentuate its appeal, offering a unique blend of relaxation and adventure.

Fort Myers Beach boasts expansive stretches of pristine white sand, seamlessly linked to the heart of the Fort Myers Beach town center. Following the devastation caused by Hurricane Ian in 2022, the community has rallied together, making commendable strides in restoration and rebuilding. The coastline is dotted with delightful dining spots and music venues, providing the perfect ambiance to savor the breathtaking sunsets over the Gulf of Mexico.

Bowditch Point Park

Nestled at the northern pinnacle of Estero Island, Bowditch Point Park seamlessly blends 17 acres of recreational and preserved areas. Its unique dual-environment offers visitors the calming Gulf beachfront on one side and the peaceful back bay waters on the other, catering to a diverse range of beach and water activities. Renowned for its captivating sunrises and sunsets, bird enthusiasts and wildlife observers often frequent the park, hoping to glimpse birds in flight or dolphins playfully navigating the waters. A series of trails crisscrossing the maritime hammock ecosystem invites explorers to immerse themselves in the region's indigenous flora and fauna. More than just a beach, Bowditch Point Park offers an environmental retreat that resonates with nature lovers. While 7 acres of the park are developed for leisurely pursuits, the remaining 10 acres stand as a testament to the area's natural beauty. Open from dawn to dusk daily, this locale beckons to those seeking both relaxation and adventure.

Address: 50 Estero Blvd, Fort Myers Beach
    Phone: (239) 823-1447
    Website: https://www.leegov.com/parks/beaches/bowditchpoint

Lovers Key Beach

Lovers Key Beach in Fort Myers was once a hidden gem, reachable only by boat. Now, it stands as one of Southwest Florida's most treasured spots, drawing beach lovers, ecologists, and couples looking for a romantic escape. Spanning four barrier islands, the park covers over 1,600 acres of untouched sandy shores, tranquil tidal inlets, and lush mangrove clusters. Activities like kayaking, paddleboarding, and canoeing allow visitors to spot manatees, dolphins, and a variety of birds, marking Lovers Key as a top destination for nature lovers. With a name that evokes passion, it's unsurprising that the park is a favorite venue for beach weddings and amorous retreats. The beach offers a perfect setting for shell enthusiasts, boasting over two miles of powdery sands against the backdrop of the Gulf of Mexico. Many are enticed by the gentle waves, ideal for swimming, snorkeling, and beachside frolics. For those interested in shelling or observing wildlife, it's a paradise. Convenient tram services run from 8:00 am to sunset, taking visitors close to the beach's expanse. Additionally, the concession stand offers rental services for paddling equipment, beach chairs, and umbrellas.

Address: 8700 Estero Blvd, Fort Myers Beach
    Phone: (239) 463-4588
    Website: https://www.floridastateparks.org/Lovers-Key

Lakes Park

Lakes Park in Fort Myers, Florida, is a scenic oasis spanning over 279 acres, offering visitors a blend of natural beauty and recreational activities. This expansive urban park features freshwater lakes, which together cover nearly 158 acres, making it a hub for water-based activities like paddle boating and kayaking. A hallmark of the park is its meandering boardwalks that traverse the lakes and wetland areas, offering close-up views of local wildlife, including various species of birds, turtles, and fish.

Families are particularly fond of the park's miniature train rides, which provide a unique and fun perspective of the park's landscape. The park also houses multiple playgrounds, ensuring children have ample space to play and explore. For those looking to stay active, Lakes Park boasts a range of fitness amenities, including well-maintained jogging and biking trails.

The park's gardens are a visual treat, especially the fragrant rose garden, which blooms vibrantly in the right seasons. In addition, several picnic shelters and rental pavilions make it an ideal spot for gatherings, birthdays, or simply enjoying a meal amidst nature. Throughout the year, Lakes Park becomes a venue for various community events and festivals, making it not just a recreational area but also a cultural hub for the residents and visitors of Fort Myers. The park is open from 7:00 am until dusk with train hours every weekend from 10:00 am to 4:00 pm. Beginning October 1st until August 9th the train will run from 10 am to 2 pm Monday thru Friday. There is a parking fee.

Address: 7330 Gladiolus Dr, Fort Myers
Phone: (239) 533-7575
Website: https://www.leegov.com/parks/parks/lakespark

Six Mile Slough Preserve

Six Mile Cypress Slough Preserve in Fort Myers, Florida, is a captivating ecological gem that spans over 3,500 acres. This freshwater wetland is teeming with life and plays a pivotal role in the regional ecosystem by acting as a natural drainage, water filtration system, and wildlife habitat.

One of the most distinguishing features of the preserve is its iconic boardwalk trail, which stretches over a mile. This raised pathway offers visitors an immersive experience as they journey through diverse habitats, ranging from wet prairies to cypress forests. Interpretative signage along the trail provides insightful information, enhancing the learning experience for nature enthusiasts.

The preserve is a haven for wildlife lovers. It's home to a myriad of species, including wading birds, alligators, turtles, otters, and even the occasional Florida panther. The dense canopy and water bodies create a serene ambiance, making it a preferred spot for birdwatchers, especially during the migratory seasons.

Six Mile Cypress Slough Preserve is also dedicated to education. The Interpretative Center on-site offers interactive exhibits about the slough's ecology, history, and the importance of wetlands in the environment. Periodic guided tours and educational programs ensure that visitors of all ages leave with a deeper appreciation and understanding of Florida's unique wetland ecosystems.

In essence, Six Mile Cypress Slough Preserve is a sanctuary of natural beauty and ecological significance, offering both recreational and educational opportunities to those who visit. It stands as a testament to Fort Myers' commitment to preserving its natural treasures for future generations. The park is open from Sunrise to Sunset. There is a parking fee.

Address: 7330 Gladiolus Dr, Fort Myers, FL
  Phone: (239) 533-7575
  Website: https://www.sloughpreserve.org/

John Yarbrough Linear Park

John Yarbrough Linear Park in Fort Myers, Florida, is a unique recreational space characterized by its elongated, linear design. Spanning six miles in length, this park is an urban greenway that offers residents and visitors an uninterrupted stretch for various activities, from walking and jogging to cycling and rollerblading.

One of the standout features of the John Yarbrough Linear Park is its multi-use path, which is paved and well-maintained, ensuring a smooth experience for users. This pathway runs parallel to the Ten Mile Canal, offering scenic water views, opportunities for bird watching, and glimpses of other local wildlife.

Bench seating at intervals provides resting spots for visitors, making it a leisurely experience for those looking to enjoy the outdoors without a rush. Given its length and its diverse landscapes, the park also serves as a corridor connecting different communities and neighborhoods in Fort Myers.

Fitness stations dotted along the trail offer a chance for more structured exercise routines, while the park's open spaces are ideal for picnics, casual ball games, or simply soaking up the Florida sun. You can ride your bike, walk, or rollerblade along the paths.

With its integration of nature and urban design, John Yarbrough Linear Park embodies the essence of a community park. It's a space that encourages physical activity, provides a serene escape from the city bustle, and fosters a sense of connectivity among Fort Myers' residents. The park is open from Sunrise to Sunset.

Address: 14608 Six Mile Cypress Parkway, Fort Myers
Phone: (239) 218-1032
Website: https://www.leegov.com/parks/parks/linearpark

BEACHES, PARKS AND WATER ACTIVITIES

11

Excursions

Fort Myers, with its serene waterways and rich ecosystems, is a paradise for kayaking enthusiasts. Embarking on a kayak excursion here promises not just physical activity but also an immersive journey into Florida's diverse natural landscape.

Setting off from a sandy shoreline, paddlers are immediately greeted by the gentle ripples of the water, reflecting the Florida sun in a dance of shimmering gold. The mangrove tunnels, iconic to this region, offer a unique paddling experience. As you glide silently beneath their arching roots and canopies, it feels like entering a different world – a quiet, green labyrinth where every turn reveals a new sight. The sound of water dripping from your paddle is often complemented by the distant calls of ospreys or the gentle rustle of the mangroves as small creatures scuttle about.

The Caloosahatchee River and Estero Bay are popular kayaking destinations in Fort Myers. Their brackish waters are home to a variety of marine life, including playful dolphins and gentle manatees. The sight of a manatee, with its slow and graceful movements, can be a mesmerizing experience, especially when viewed from the intimate perspective of a kayak.

Beyond the thrill of wildlife encounters, kayaking in Fort Myers also offers a lesson in ecology. The region's estuaries play a crucial role in maintaining the balance of the local ecosystem. As you paddle, the changing landscapes—from open water to dense mangroves—tell a story of nature's adaptability and resilience.

Wrapping up a kayak excursion as the sun sets over Fort Myers is magical. The horizon is painted in hues of orange, pink, and purple, the waters mirror the candy-colored skies, and the world seems to slow down for a moment. With each stroke taking you closer to the shore, there's a profound sense of gratitude—for the beauty of nature and the simple joys of kayaking in such a pristine environment.

There are several places that you can rent Kayak's and explore the area. A couple of our favorite places are listed below. The tours were awesome.

Kayak Excursions – Bunche Beach
Address: 17950 John Morris Rd, Fort Myers
Phone: (239) 297-7011
Website: https://kayak-excursions.com/

Lovers Key Adventures & Events
Address: 8700 Estero Blvd, Fort Myers Beach
Phone: (239) 765-7788
Website: https://www.loverskeyadventures.com/

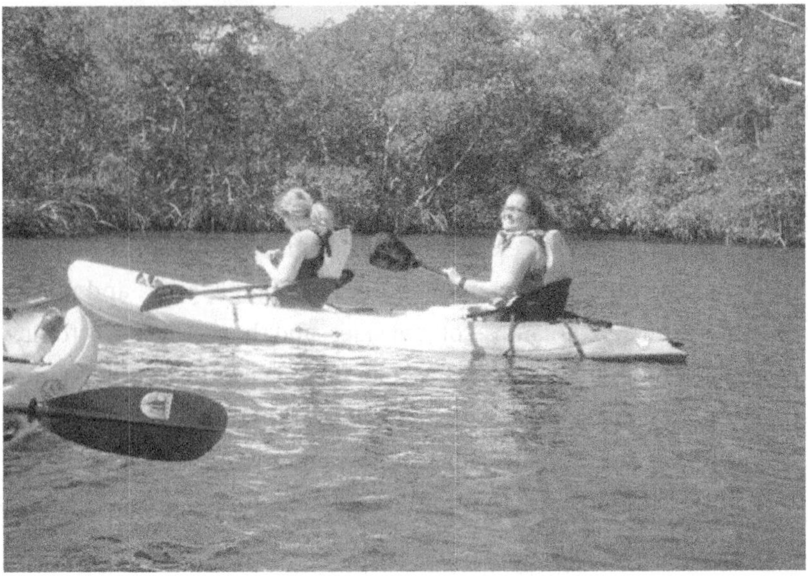

12

Boat Rental, Jet Ski Rentals and Boat Charters

Your Boat Club (Boat rental)
   Address: 18650 San Carlos Blvd, Fort Myers Beach
   Phone: (612) 208-1800
Website: https://yourboatclub.com

Salty Sam's Marina (Boat rentals and storage)
   Address: 2500 Main Street, Fort Myers Beach
   Phone: (239) 463-7333
   Website: https://www.saltysamsmarina.com/

Sunset Jet Ski Rental & Tours (Jet Skis and Fishing Charters)
   Address: 18276 Cutlass Dr, Fort Myers Beach
   Phone: (239) 880-7929
   Website: https://sunsetjsr.com/

All Island Watersports (Jet Skis, Parasailing, Boat tours, and more)

Address: 61 Avenue C, Fort Myers Beach
Phone: (239) 765-1284
Website: https://theislandwatersports.com/

13

Entertainment and Activities

Barbara B. Mann Performing Arts Hall

Located in Fort Myers, Florida, the Barbara B. Mann Performing Arts Hall stands as a cultural beacon for the arts and entertainment community. As the foremost venue for performances in the region, it boasts state-of-the-art facilities that cater to a broad spectrum of events ranging from Broadway shows, orchestras, and ballets to popular music concerts and comedic acts.

With a seating capacity that accommodates thousands, the hall is designed for optimal acoustics and offers an intimate viewing experience, ensuring that every seat provides a clear view of the stage. The interior is characterized by plush seating, elegant décor, and a warm ambiance that resonates with the rich cultural performances it hosts.

Over the years, the Barbara B. Mann Performing Arts Hall has been the venue of choice for various touring companies, renowned musicians, and top-tier theatrical productions. Its reputation extends beyond just the local community; it's recognized in the broader performing arts industry as a premier location in Southwest Florida.

Beyond the performances, the venue is known for its outstanding hospitality. The friendly staff, well-maintained amenities, and convenient location make it a favorite among patrons.

In essence, the Barbara B. Mann Performing Arts Hall is more than just a performance venue; it's a cornerstone of Fort Myers' cultural landscape, providing residents and visitors with enriching experiences and unforgettable memories.

Address: 13350 FSW Parkway, Fort Myers
Phone: (239) 481-4849
Website: https://www.bbmannpah.com/

Broadway Palm

Broadway Palm, situated in the heart of Fort Myers, Florida, is a celebrated dinner theater that masterfully combines fine dining with top-tier theatrical productions. Since its inception, it has become a staple in the region's entertainment scene, drawing both locals and tourists seeking a unique and memorable evening out.

Upon entering, patrons are immediately greeted by an elegant setting that hints at the dual delights of gourmet cuisine and captivating performances. The dining experience at Broadway Palm is a treat in itself, with a diverse menu that caters to a variety of tastes, complemented by a well-curated selection of beverages. The culinary offerings often set the tone for the evening, priming guests for the entertainment to follow.

The theater itself boasts state-of-the-art acoustics and lighting, ensuring that each production is showcased in the best possible light. With a varied repertoire that includes classic Broadway hits, musicals, comedies, and seasonal specials, Broadway Palm consistently delivers performances that resonate with a wide audience demographic. The talented casts, often comprising seasoned professionals and budding stars, bring stories to life on stage with passion and flair.

Beyond the main stage, Broadway Palm also features the Off Broadway Palm Theatre, a secondary space dedicated to smaller, more intimate productions and events, expanding the range of artistic offerings available to patrons.

In essence, Broadway Palm is more than just a theater; it's an institution in Fort Myers that celebrates the joy of live performances and the communal experience of sharing a meal. It stands as a testament to the city's vibrant arts scene and its commitment to providing residents and visitors with diverse, high-quality entertainment options.

Address: 1380 Colonial Blvd, Fort Myers
Phone: (239) 278-4422
Website: https://broadwaypalm.com/

Murder Mystery Dinner Train

The Murder Mystery Dinner Train offers an intriguing fusion of gourmet dining and interactive theater, all set against the backdrop of a scenic train journey. As the train glides along the tracks, passengers are not only treated to a sumptuous meal but also become part of a thrilling whodunit tale that unfolds right before their eyes.

Upon boarding, guests are immediately immersed in a captivating storyline, set in a bygone era or a specific theme, where suspicious characters and intricate plots weave a tapestry of mystery. As courses are served, clues are subtly revealed, and the plot thickens. Passengers become both spectators and detectives, piecing together hints, interacting with the characters, and often even becoming part of the story themselves.

The dining experience is crafted to match the caliber of the performance. With a meticulously curated menu, guests are treated to multiple courses, each dish prepared with attention to detail, ensuring a delightful culinary journey that complements the unfolding drama.

One of the unique aspects of the Murder Mystery Dinner Train is the moving scenery. As the mystery deepens inside the train, outside, landscapes change, offering panoramic views that add another layer of ambiance to the entire experience. By the journey's end, as dessert plates are cleared and the mystery reaches its climax, guests are encouraged to share their deductions and guess the culprit. The big reveal is always a moment of suspense, surprise, and often, amusement. It is a fun adventure and a must-experience.

Address: 2805 Colonial Blvd, Fort Myers
Phone: (239) 275-8487
Website: https://semgulf.com/

OTHER ACTIVITIES

There are so many other events that are always going on in our area. Here are some other ideas and events that you can visit while you are here.

Edison Festival of Lights

The Edison Festival of Lights in Fort Myers, Florida, is an iconic annual event that pays tribute to the town's most famous winter resident, Thomas Edison. Celebrated in February to honor Edison's birthday, the festival has grown over the decades into one of Southwest Florida's most anticipated and vibrant events. Rooted in a tradition that dates back to the 1930s, the festival not only celebrates the inventor's remarkable contributions to science and innovation but also showcases the rich cultural tapestry and community spirit of Fort Myers.

A highlight of the festival is the dazzling Grand Parade, which attracts over 200,000 spectators each year. This nighttime spectacle is a cascade of illuminated floats, marching bands, dancers, and performers, all weaving through the streets in a symphony of light and sound. Beyond the parade, the festival encompasses a plethora of activities, including a 5K run, a junior parade, and the glamorous Coronation Ball. Craft fairs, car shows, and concerts further add to the festivities, making the Edison Festival of Lights not just a tribute to a legendary inventor, but also a celebration of community, culture, and the enduring power of human ingenuity.

Their website is: https://www.edisonfestival.org/

Downtown Fort Myers – Music Walk, Art Walk, Tree lighting, Fireworks & more

Downtown Fort Myers, with its historic charm and riverside beauty, transforms into a cultural hotspot on designated evenings, hosting a series of vibrant events that highlight the city's rich arts and entertainment scene. At the heart of this cultural renaissance are the beloved Music Walk and Art Walk events, which draw residents and visitors alike, eager to experience the city's creative pulse.

The Art Walk, typically held on the first Friday of each month, is a visual treat for art aficionados. Galleries and art spaces open their doors to showcase a diverse array of artworks, from contemporary paintings and sculptures to intricate crafts and photography. As attendees stroll the cobblestone streets, they can interact with local artists, engage in art demonstrations, and even purchase unique pieces to add to their collections. The atmosphere is enhanced by live street performances and the aromas from nearby cafes and restaurants, making it a multisensory experience.

On the third Friday, the Music Walk takes center stage, turning downtown Fort Myers into a musical haven. Live bands, solo artists, and DJs fill the air with melodies from various genres—jazz, blues, rock, and more. The streets come alive as spontaneous dance areas emerge, and patrons are invited to sing along, tap their feet, or simply soak in the eclectic tunes. Beyond these signature events, downtown also hosts themed festivals, seasonal markets, and theatrical performances, solidifying its reputation as Fort Myers' cultural and entertainment epicenter. Each event, be it Music Walk, Art Walk, or any other, underscores the city's commitment to fostering community ties, celebrating artistic talents, and offering memorable experiences to all.

Centennial Park, nestled in the heart of Fort Myers, stands as a verdant oasis amidst the city's urban landscape. Stretching along the banks of

ENTERTAINMENT AND ACTIVITIES

the Caloosahatchee River, this picturesque park offers a tranquil retreat with its expansive lawns, shady trees, and meandering pathways. A favorite among locals and visitors alike, the park features amenities like a playground for children, picnic areas, and a fishing pier. Moreover, its riverside location provides stunning views, especially during sunset, making it a popular spot for relaxation, recreation, and community gatherings.

Here is a website with some information - https://www.myriverdistrict.com/

14

Shopping

Edison Mall

Edison Mall, located in the bustling city of Fort Myers, Florida, stands as one of the region's premier shopping destinations. With its rich history, it has been a staple in the community for decades, offering residents and visitors a blend of retail, dining, and entertainment options with over 130 shops and restaurants.

Spanning a vast expanse, the mall boasts a diverse array of stores, from nationally recognized brands to unique local boutiques, catering to a wide range of tastes and budgets. Whether you're in search of the latest fashion trends, tech gadgets, or simply everyday essentials, Edison Mall is a one-stop shopping haven.

Beyond retail, Edison Mall is home to a variety of dining establishments. Foodies can indulge in a selection of eateries, ranging from casual fast-food outlets to sit-down restaurants offering a more refined dining experience. The food court, often buzzing with activity, provides a quick and convenient option for those looking to grab a bite in between shopping.

The mall's architecture and design reflect a blend of modern aesthetics and functional spaces. Wide, well-lit corridors, comfortable seating areas, and strategic store placements ensure a pleasant shopping experience for all. Regular events, promotions, and seasonal festivities make the mall a vibrant hub of activity, drawing crowds and fostering a sense of community. In essence, Edison Mall in Fort Myers isn't just a shopping center; it's a gathering place, a nexus of commerce and culture, where memories are made, and experiences are shared. Its enduring presence in the community speaks to its adaptability and commitment to serving the evolving needs of its patrons.

Address: 4125 Cleveland Ave, Fort Myers
Phone: (239) 939-5464
Website: https://shopedisonmall.com/

Miromar Outlets

Miromar Outlets is located just south of Fort Myers in Estero, Florida, stands as a premier shopping destination for those in search of top brands at unbeatable prices. This expansive outdoor mall boasts over 140 designer and brand-name outlets, offering a diverse range of apparel, accessories, home goods, and more. Set against a backdrop of Mediterranean architecture, reflective water features, and elegantly landscaped courtyards, the shopping experience is elevated by the mall's serene and inviting ambiance. Beyond retail therapy, Miromar Outlets offers a range of dining options, from quick bites to sit-down restaurants, catering to various culinary preferences. Regular events, promotions, and entertainment activities further enhance the vibrant atmosphere, making Miromar Outlets not just a shopping hub, but also a social and recreational centerpiece in Estero.

Address: 10801 Corkscrew Rd, Estero
Phone: (239) 948-3766
Website: https://miromaroutlets.com/

GulfCoast Town Center

Gulf Coast Town Center, located in Fort Myers, Florida, is more than just a shopping complex; it's a sprawling epicenter of retail, dining, and entertainment. Spread over a vast area, this open-air center seamlessly blends a diverse range of stores, from popular high-street brands to unique boutiques, ensuring a shopping experience that caters to every preference and budget. Beyond its extensive retail offerings, the center is a gastronomic haven, with many restaurants, cafes, and eateries offering cuisines from around the world. Whether you're in the mood for a gourmet meal, a quick snack, or a refreshing beverage, there's something to satiate every palate. But the allure of Gulf Coast Town Center doesn't end with shopping and dining. The venue frequently buzzes with entertainment options, including a state-of-the-art cinema, live music events, and seasonal festivals. Its beautifully landscaped plazas, complete with fountains and seating areas, provide the perfect backdrop for a leisurely day out or a night of fun. In essence, Gulf Coast Town Center stands as a testament to modern-day leisure, where shopping, dining, and entertainment converge to offer a holistic experience for residents and visitors alike. If you are looking to see a movie, there is Regal Cinemas. You will find Bass Pro Shops, PF Chang's China Bistro, Costco, Target, and many more.

Address: 9903 Gulf Coast Main Street, Fort Myers
Phone: (239) 267-5107
Website: https://www.gulfcoasttowncenter.com/

Coconut Point Mall

Coconut Point Mall, situated in the picturesque Estero, Florida, is a shopper's paradise and a focal point for both leisure and luxury. Spanning a vast expanse, this open-air mall boasts a curated collection of over 100 stores, ranging from high-end designer boutiques to popular retail chains, ensuring a shopping experience that's both diverse and delightful. Its elegant Mediterranean-inspired architecture, combined with lush landscaping and serene water features, enhances the overall ambiance, making every visit a visual treat. Beyond shopping, Coconut Point offers an array of dining options, catering to a myriad of tastes, be it gourmet eateries or cozy cafes. Regular events, promotions, and entertainment offerings further invigorate the mall's lively atmosphere.

Whether you're indulging in some retail therapy, enjoying a sumptuous meal, or simply taking a leisurely stroll, Coconut Point Mall stands as Estero's premier destination for fashion, food, and fun.

Address: 23106 Fashion Dr, Estero, FL
   Phone: (239) 992-4259
   Website: https://www.simon.com/mall/coconut-point

15

Resources

All the resources utilized for this travel guide can be found footnoted, complete with their respective websites, on individual pages.

16

Conclusion

As we draw our journey through Fort Myers and Fort Myers Beach to a close, it's evident that this corner of Florida is more than just a vacation destination; it's a symphony of vibrant cultures, rich history, natural wonders, and unforgettable experiences. From the tranquil waters of the Gulf to the bustling streets of downtown Fort Myers, every moment spent here promises memories that last a lifetime.

Having walked alongside you through this guide, I hope I've illuminated the many treasures that await your discovery. Whether you're a first-time visitor or a returning traveler, there's always something new to explore, a hidden gem to uncover. As you embark on your own adventures, may you find the same enchantment in these locales as I have.

If this guide has enriched your travels or provided valuable insights, I kindly ask that you consider leaving a review. Your feedback not only helps fellow travelers but also aids in refining future editions of this guide. Let's continue to celebrate and share the magic of Fort Myers and Fort Myers Beach, ensuring that its charm is experienced by many generations to come. Safe travels and until next time!

Made in the USA
Coppell, TX
06 July 2024